25 NOTES
for the
Successful
Musician.
©

D0985893

For more information, please visit 25notes.com

25 NOTES

for the
Successful
Musician©

The Ultimate Guide to **MAKING IT**
in the Music Industry

Chad Jeffers

Published by Groovenslide, Franklin, Tennessee.

Groovenslide also publishes its books in a variety of electronic formats. Some content that appears in print may not be available in electronic books. For more information about Groovenslide products, visit our website at www.25notes.com

Library of Congress Cataloging-in-Publication Data:
Jeffers, Chad L
25 Notes for the Successful Musician

Printed in the United States of America.

This book is dedicated to

my family and friends who

have helped me on my journey.

Author's Biography

You wouldn't think a musician who's played behind Keith Urban, Carrie Underwood and Kenny Loggins, among others, would have made any mistakes along the way or second-guessed himself as he went along. But Chad Jeffers says that the road to success is paved with plenty of pitfalls, and knowing the ropes beforehand could have saved him a lot of time.

That's why Chad, a highly-respected guitarist, dobro and pedal steel player with worldwide tours and years of experience under his belt, has authored *25 Notes for the Successful Musician*, a self-help book packed with practical advice and guidelines for aspiring musicians — novice or seasoned.

"It's basically everything I've learned in the last 15 years that I wish I would've known when I started out," Jeffers explains.

25 Notes (25notes.com) is a valuable compendium of step-by-step information for musicians at each stage of their career.

"There are things in my book that I've never found on the Internet or in any other book," he explains. "I think people can actually save five years (or more) of their professional life with *25 Notes*, because it gives an in-depth look at how the music business really works. It takes the gloves off — there's no sugar coating on anything. It's everything I've learned or been taught by the musicians I've worked with."

After high school, Jeffers moved to Nashville to attend Belmont University where he later would receive a scholarship where he double-majored in music business and marketing.

Through the years of playing with renowned musicians and artists, it is time for the knowledge to be passed on.

"People always tell me that I'm living the dream," Jeffers says. "I've been blessed to play with world-class vocalists and musicians, people who are truly the best of the best, and they've given me a sense of pride in my own work. But now that I'm moving into a different chapter in my life with producing, songwriting and authoring this book, it's important to me to take everything I've learned and pass it along. If others hadn't helped me in my journey, I wouldn't be here today. My hope is that aspiring musicians will read this, take it to heart and practice what they've read. And one day, maybe they'll write their own book to inspire the next generation. To me, that's what living the dream is really all about."

By Kip Kirby

Table of Contents

Foreword
(by Chad Kroeger of Nickelback)

So do you think you have what it takes to be a professional musician? Do you think it is all about partying, staying up late and being irresponsible? Maybe some of that is true, but there is more to the story. It is not an easy business. People will dump on you, tell lies to your face and be a plain jerk to you. However, those who learn to deal with and overcome it and become the bigger person come out on top.

The music business has its benefits and is so rewarding! During my career, I've been fortunate to reap many of those benefits and rewards. But, Nickelback worked very hard to achieve what many may say is an "overnight success." Hardly anything in this business is an overnight success. We worked for years together as a band, fine-tuning our sound and image to become what people know today as "Nickelback." Even now we are very active in writing, recording and producing our live show. Sure, we have many talented and creative people around us who help us be great at what we do, but we have ownership in our success. We work really hard; that's half the fun!

Being in the music business takes methodical hard work and planning. And sometimes, it just takes some plain luck to get the chance to claim your stake in the business. Once you get the chance, run like hell with it because you probably won't get a second one. If you are lucky enough to get a break, take it and seriously work it hard!

To be a professional musician you will have good days and bad. But in the end it is so worth it.

Whether you are a singer or a musician, write! Not only is your "voice" heard, but writing also helps define you as an artist.

Use *25 Notes for the Successful Musician* as your guide to help you in this crazy business called music. The words Chad writes will help you be successful. But, you must follow through. Just reading this book only gives you knowledge; you need applied knowledge to succeed.

May you have a wonderful career in music and always keep pushing forward.

Best of luck in your music career and never give up.

Rock on!

Chad Kroeger

Author's Acknowledgements

Thanks to my amazing wife, Suzanne, my support and lifeline. I love you. I can't leave out our "wonder dog," Sebastian. He was with me through writing almost this entire book. He would just stare, but I know he's taking it all in.

To my mom and dad, who have always supported me in my music. Sometimes I think my decisions didn't make complete sense to them, but they still stuck by me — from the days when I was eight years old and just learning to play different instruments, to backing up my father as he would entertain folks with his beautiful voice and guitar. Dad, you have always been and continue to be an inspiration to me, and it's because of you that I can do music for a living. I am eternally grateful.

To my brother Michael and his lovely wife, Caron. You guys are the best! Michael, through the years, it has always been fun making music. We've had some great moments!

Mr. And Mrs. Lee Bradford, I truly appreciate you welcoming me to your family. Your love and support means so much to me.

To Jimmy Olander, I'm so glad I got the nerve to come up to you all of those years ago and start a conversation. Your mentoring has helped me beyond imagination, both personally and professionally. You are such a dear friend. This book is a reflection of your guidance.

Toni Rufo, Diane Sheets and Danny Memeo... you all keep me laughing all the time and you have always been such a great sounding board for all of my crazy ideas. I'm so glad you're in my life!

When it came time to put this book and my website together, Melissa Behring was the first one who really rattled my cage. Melissa, I couldn't have done it without you. You and Jake are the best.

Mattie Gallagher, you are a miracle worker! Thank you for coming in at the 4th quarter of this project and really making it great! I look forward to more projects with you.

Ryan Brown. Simple and brilliant. When it comes to graphics, you completely read my mind. All of my logos and of course the cover of "25 Notes for the Successful Musician," are beyond my expectations. You truly are talented, my friend.

To Don Cusic, who years ago over coffee really gave me this idea that I could actually do this. Cusic was my professor when I was in school, and is obviously still schoolin' me! Thank you for the inspiration and guidance.

To all the musicians and artists, past and present, that I've had the honor to perform with. All of you have been such an encouraging force to my music. I've been so blessed to have played (and still play) with the best in the business!

Thanks be to God for the talent and drive He blesses me with everyday. The Master of all Creation.

Note 1: This Is What It's All About!

"**Five** minutes!" is yelled into our dressing room as we are preparing to entertain approximately 14,000 people. Currently, I'm on tour with one of the hottest music acts in the world. The dressing room is quiet, but you can hear the rumbling of the building as concertgoers are getting to their seats and getting settled. There is energy about the physical building, almost as if "it" is going to perform. As a band, we circle up and say a prayer. We give thanks for our talents, strengths, and ask that we reach the people tonight, especially those who may need a little extra attention for whatever struggle they may be facing in their life. After prayer, we usually do one last "pit stop" and then head to the stage. While going to the stage, we keep it lighthearted and fun, usually pickin' at one another or sharing a joke or story about something that happened that day. We also check our in-ear monitor pack to make sure we have batteries and signal.

Once I get to side stage and meet up with my guitar tech, he usually tells me about anything out of the ordinary. I've been blessed to have some of the best guitar techs that have walked the earth. They make a musician's job so much easier — we just focus on playing and performing. I do not worry about whether a guitar has been tuned or is working. As I put on my guitar, the house lights go out. There is a huge roar from the crowd. While all this commotion is going on, I'm stretching my hands and arms and warming up.

I check my ear pack once again. Since our monitor guy is close, he usually briefs us on the wireless conditions for the night. In larger cities, there are so many frequencies swirling in the air it sometimes does a number on our ear packs. If so, it will sound a bit fuzzy. Sometimes we'll take "hits." A hit is a very loud "slam--pop!" which makes it feel like you just lost your hearing.

As the crowd starts to clap in unison, the pre-show video rolls. We have our stage entrance timed perfectly. Once set with the opening tune, as a final check I give all my equipment a visual once-over to make sure pedals are on the right setting, guitar picks are out and the cables are plugged in. I can still hear the crowd, even though I have my in ear monitors in. As the pre-show film comes to an end, I can feel the excitement and tension, and my heart's thumpin' as the count-off is heard only to the band. We launch into the first tune!

As a musician, it is part of the job to be excited. However, it is also your job to do your part. You don't want to "rush" musically, so the first verse and chorus of the show are the most tense. This is when I look through the crowd to see if there's anyone I know. Usually, we can see the first five to eight rows pretty well. We also look to see who the show's partiers are going to be. It's best to make these connections early in the show. If you don't, you'll probably have a harder time connecting to your audience. For those people you can't see through the lights, the trick is to look through the arena for the exit signs. Honestly! I learned this trick a long time ago. If you smile and "interact" with the exit signs, you will connect with many people in that area who you can't even see. (Now that my secret is out, I'm busted!)

After the second or third song, I am usually settled in and ready for the pacing of the show. With many tours, the artist will do a few songs acoustically by him or herself. This is usually our time to make any fine adjustments with our gear or monitors. It is always a good idea to interact with your fellow musicians on stage. It makes every show dynamic and fun. Plus, we usually see something funny either on stage or in the audience that will make us laugh. We see so many funny and quite colorful actions from the crowd; it almost makes me feel guilty that I didn't pay to get into the show!

> *"The opportunity of a lifetime is only relevant during the lifetime of the opportunity! So work hard and dare to dream, have the courage to follow your heart. Be prepared, as you will never know when it comes a knocking!"*
> — *Ben Carey of Lifehouse (Artist/Musician)*

Note 2: When the Show is Over

Last song before the encore, we catch our second wind. We know the show will be over soon, so the band is giving it our all. After the last note of the tune (pre-encore), we go back stage, grab some water and talk about the night's show. Usually one of the band members tells something funny he saw in the crowd, like commenting about the older couple that held their ears throughout the whole show. If you are sensitive to loud noise, why sit in the front at a concert of that magnitude with no ear protection, when you know it's going to be loud?

As the crowd keeps getting louder and louder, we get the "Okay! Let's go!" As an encore for most shows, we do two, maybe three songs. When I was out with Urban and the crowd was really into it, he'd play as many cover tunes as he could (before the curfew). Curfew is what the promoter and building have set as the absolute time the show must be over. On our last show of the tour, the stage was not going to be used anymore. Keith had the crew come out and literally cut it up. It was made from a Styrofoam material. They handed it out to the crowd while we played another 45 minutes or so of covers! Pretty crazy! It's been said that we played too long, that they had to pay fines and so forth because of the local union! Ha... Rock'n Roll.

Once the last note of the last encore song is played, we all congregate in the dressing room. Most of the dressing rooms have nice furniture, where you can sit and relax, hang out for a bit and put our ear monitors away.

Back in the days when we had to strike our own gear, which I still do when I am part of USO shows or "sub" for fellow musicians. It is noteworthy to mention that you are there to be the entertainer, so sell it even after you leave the stage. *Yes,* the stage needs to be "striked," but if it is possible to wait until the room has been cleared, it will keep you shining in the light of the performer.

Many times if we are giggin' in a bar or social setting like that, we'll go out and hang with the fans. It means a lot to them and it gives you a chance to chill out for a bit and probably hear some crazy fan stories. Or you may be going to the merchandise table to sell and sign your merchandise.

If you must strike the stage immediately, I've seen guys throw on a different shirt. 1.) It saves your show shirt, and 2.) sometimes the fan doesn't recognize you. After striking, put your show shirt on and go socialize. By doing this, for many fans it will make you and your band appear to be "*The Entertainer.*" I learned this lesson the hard way... I used to rush to tear all of my equipment down. Fans would yell for me to come over and sign something, so while holding pedals and cables, I'd try to be a rock star and appease them. It was awkward for all of us. I'm on the stage leaning over trying to get pictures with them and sign while my hands were literally full.

If the drive is a long one, many will take a quick shower and clean up. It is not desirable to be sweaty, smellin', and nasty for an 18-hour bus ride. Usually when we get back to the bus the Production Assistant has already been on the bus and brought after-show food. Many times, they'll get the food from a local restaurant. Sometimes it is great... sometimes it is not. After about 30 minutes, our driver is on the scene prepping the bus for the overnight drive. We go to the next town and the next hotel. Maybe take a nap, wake up at around 3:00 a.m., go into the hotel and do it all over again!

Another day down.

> "*I guess the first thing that comes to mind would be to young artists and players. That they would work hard to find their own individual voice and have the courage to express it just the way they feel it and hear it. Avoid comparison to other players/artists at all cost. We are all created one-of-a-kind, and no one else can be you. So, be you.*"
> — *Gene Miller (Musician)*

Note 3: Playing when you don't feel like it

What truly separates the amateurs from the pros is the answer to this question: When you feel sick, are you too sick to play? I've seen guys play some of their best shows when they were sick. On one show, I remember a drummer actually had a trashcan next to his drum kit... just in case. But it was one of his best performances.

Personally, I only had one show where I was sick. The night before, I ate some food that gave me food poisoning. Before the show, the artist encouraged me on, by advising that there are only 12,000 people watching me. "Try not to puke" were her words of wisdom. I made it, but there were some moments that didn't look too promising. It's funny that we recently did a show and this artist was sick and had cans on the sides of the stage!

This also applies to practicing. Many times as a professional musician, you'll wake up in the morning knowing you must practice, but you would rather sleep. Know that there are a million other people just waiting for your spot. In other words, get your butt out of bed and practice.

> *"Some days I would be worn out, but I still went to work. While sitting at my drum set, right before the 'red light' would be lit, I would tell myself, 'Whatever I play in this moment, in this time and space, has the potential to last forever. So play with all of your heart and soul, because Records are Forever'."*
> — *Craig Krampf (Musician/AFM Secretary-Treasurer), referencing his days as an L.A. session drummer*

When learning a new artist's show, don't wait until the last minute. It will bite you every single time. Have a system you can go by. My system is listening to every song and getting an idea of the set. Chart each song out individually. Go back and start learning parts. Then practice the song in its entirety. Another helpful hint, if you have the gear for it, which you should, record yourself practicing.

When I was prepping for the Loggins tour, they sent me tracks of all the music on one side and my parts on the other. It was very helpful and allowed me to record my practice sessions and compare them to the original. Recording also allows you to dial in your tone and settings. Everyone has his or her own method and you should have yours.

"When dealing with a bleak turn out gig (Perhaps the band is close to outnumbering the crowd? Everyone raise their hands if you've done this gig? Liars!), remember these are the people who "did" come. It's bad form to treat them like the ones that blew you off."
— Jimmy Olander (Artist/Musician)

Note 4: Award Shows

I'm writing this from our suite in the Staples Center. We are performing tonight on the 50th annual Grammy Awards Show. We have been in L.A. for the past four days for rehearsals, and this morning we had a complete run through of the show. The actual broadcast will start at 5:00 p.m. Pacific.

People often ask what it is like to play on awards and/or TV shows. Most of the time, there is a lot of hurry and wait. For instance, we left the hotel this morning at 8:30 a.m., played at 10:15 a.m., and now wait until the show starts at 5:00 p.m. This is a great time for me to write!

For the musicians, award shows can be challenging. A few factors come into play. You have to be able to "dial" in your tone, tune your instrument, and make all of your adjustments fairly quickly. NOTE: In these situations, it is always good to know your equipment well. Usually when you rent gear, you have your options of the brand/model you desire. Having something you know helps dramatically in these tense situations. You are typically hitting the stage cold. There are no warm ups or settling in. It is simply, go plug in and the cameras are on, and then you perform. Once you hit the stage for both rehearsal and the show, it's a rush.

Even though it can be challenging, there are so many benefits! First of all, you are getting TV money, which may pay you residually. That means you will be paid every time the show is aired around the world. Many call it mailbox money. I have gone to my P.O. Box and had a "normal" day turn into a very a big payday! As a matter of fact, as I'm putting the final touches on this book, I received 2 checks today. Maybe that is why I'm in such a good mood! There is no feeling like that in the world. Once you experience it, you'll never forget it. Award shows also allow you to see many of your friends and make new ones. At the Grammys, you honestly ride elevators, pass in the halls or eat lunch in catering with some of your musical heroes.

This brings up a good point about seeing some well-known musicians and artists. There is a fine line between "gherming" someone (being an over-zealous fan) and being professional. The timing and the situation determine much of it. If the person is pre-occupied and clearly not in a situation to be approached, the timing is not right and it is best to let the moment pass and hope for another chance. If the timing seems right, you may benefit from the experience. Benefits may include inspiration in many facets of your life, helping your career, or as just down right bragging rights.

Many times when you perform on other shows such as The Tonight Show and Saturday Night Live, you may briefly be able to meet the host and guests. Sometimes it is during the show live on TV. It's always nice to meet those folks. When we performed on Saturday Night Live, it was a rush to meet Tina Fey and the cast, as well as the Saturday Night Live Band. Even if you've just met them briefly, your friends may think you hung out with them all day long, unless you tell them otherwise.

"There is no substitution for listening and playing only what is needed. Here, and really anywhere, the old saying 'less is more' is very true. I play for artists telling a story. No one wants to have two storytellers telling two stories at the same time."
— *Brian Oaks (Producer/Musician)*

Note 5: Being Signed and Dropped as an Artist to a Major Label

One of the most memorable eras of my life was being in a country band, Pinmonkey, and being signed to RCA. It was also one of the most frustrating times. When you are in a band, you feel so passionate about your music; you expect the world to react the same way. That rarely happens, and it was definitely an eye opener for me. However, we did have some die-hard fans, known as "Pinmonkey Junkies." They really supported the band and got us through many tough times. When some radio would refuse to play our songs or when something happened business wise, we could hit the stage and look out and see familiar faces, and that made it all worthwhile. Some of the "junkies" would travel hundreds of miles to catch a show. Others would even travel with us, much like Grateful Dead's Deadheads. I'm telling you all of this because it really made us feel like our music mattered, and sometimes it was a key force in keeping our spirits up while on the road.

It is crucial to have meaning and purpose behind your music. Some artists say it in their lyrics in an effort to make political statements or offer content relevant to present culture. Others will go as far from that as they can and just have "fun, feel good" music. And then of course there are the romantics. I fall more on the romanticism side. I want my music to be fun and also have a purpose. I've learned you can't have all serious songs, and it isn't a good idea to have all fun/lighthearted tunes. But we are talking about belief and how you feel about your music. If you don't believe in your music, regardless of what it is, you will give up. No matter who you are, you will have tough times and tough decisions to make. All of that makes the good times so much sweeter. When you witness fans at your show singing along to your song and having the time of their life, you're aware of the greater purpose of music. When one of your favorite artists comes up to you after a show and praises your performance, it is an extraordinary feeling! When you walk into a radio station to try and get your song added to their play list, and the Program Director says, "I'll never play this band on my station," it is an exhilarating feeling when you win them over. This actually happened to us. We pulled out our guitars and won him over in two songs! He took us immediately to the on-air DJ and told him to put us on the air "Right Now!" True story!

But as the saying goes, "All good things must come to an end." As a band, we were sitting at our manager's conference table while he finished up some work. We were in the middle of cutting a new album, so we were talking about songs, the first single (which had already been released), album photo shoots, who we would like to tour with and plotting out a marketing plan. Generally, artist marketing plans consist of strategies for touring and self-promotion, and they sometimes come with additional label support. Our manager, Rick Alter, walked into the room and said he just spoke with RCA's President, Joe Galante. Rick went on to say that he was informed we would not be moving forward with the single, or the album. We would not even be moving forward with the project. There was an awkward silence. We all just sat there and stared at each other. Then someone said, "So did we just get dropped?" "Yeah." I always wondered what it would feel like to get dropped from a major label, and it happened. It wasn't at all how I thought it would feel. As a band, we were in recording mode, so we collectively decided to immediately start a new project. So in a way, it was actually a sense of relief. Cutting an album independently and having full control of it alleviated some of the major label pressures. But with that also came more responsibility on our parts. We were all parts of the puzzle. Any mistakes, the blame would be on us! Also, we did not get an advance to help support us financially while making the album… oh yeah… and also *no recording budget*. But we pulled favors and created an album that to this day I am still proud of. Mark Bright, who produced the tracks we were cutting for RCA, told our manager he wanted to be a part of the independent album. His feelings were that he signed on to produce Pinmonkey because of us, not because we were signed to a major label.

Note 6: Everything Happens for a Reason

Throughout my career, I have worked hard not to burn any bridges. Sometimes that is much easier said than done. If you do your best and are professional, hopefully you can get out of sticky situations and be able to move forward. Looking back, even some of the rough situations I've been in have mended and have spawned new lives. There are always the gigs you take that are not the best situations. Sometimes it is rough living conditions, while other times it's a strange chemistry between band members. I've been on gigs where the spouse is on the bus with us, which may create some interesting bus rides. When I took a gig with Jamie O'Neal, the first night I ever played with her, they asked, "Are you going?" I had no idea what they were talking about. I said, 'Going where?" She said, "We are going to Iraq, go with us!" So that was an interesting call to my wife that night. But she was able to go as well and we had a great time! One year later, I received another call to go back with Granger Smith. It was a life-changing trip for me! The first trip, everything was taken care of; this trip, we were loading our gear every day and flying by helicopter to different locations. On the last night, flying over Baghdad, we had two missiles lock on us. I was sitting on the door seat (which there were no doors). Flares were shooting out of the chopper to deflect the potential RPG missiles locked on us.

Also, plant seeds with individuals you meet along the way, because you never know what will grow into a new opportunity. As for my career, many "definites" were not so definite, but the pipe dreams actually turned into reality.

The music business is a small, tight-knit community. While writing this, I was interrupted by a phone call from a guy in L.A. whom I have never met. I stumbled onto his website earlier this morning. He is a session drummer who is doing a lot of recording by leveraging the Internet. This has also recently become my personal focus. I emailed him through his website to brainstorm and collaborate on some of his ideas about marketing this unique service online. We play different instruments, so there is no concern over competition. Over the course of our conversation, I found out one of his past roommates is in the touring band I'm in right now!

Like in life, many times something perceived as negative can actually be a blessing in disguise. Bottom line is keeping a positive attitude and always being on the look out for an opportunity. Do your due diligence in planning and plotting your next move. Write down all of your goals and dreams and see how it can transform your life.

"Be a great player, wear your passion on your sleeve, be over-prepared for every gig, be confident, be happy, be well dressed, be on time (be early), have great gear, have a firm hand shake, look people in the eye, remember names, do what you say you are going to do, have a business card, have a website, have a demo reel, have promotional materials, go beyond expectations always, deliver, and have fun!"
— Rich Redmond (Musician)

Note 7: If I Moved to 'Town' with $500 in my Pocket

I've seen many people come through town and either have success in the music business or get chewed up and spit out. From watching both sides, this is what I learned. By the way, this is based on an assignment from my college professor at Belmont University, the late David Skepner.

What would you do if you showed up to town with a guitar on your back, a suitcase and some living money in your pocket?

The first step is survival! You must find an affordable place to live and find a job. *Any* kind of job! But this is only the starting point. For me, I always tried to find jobs that were either directly or indirectly involved with my music. Many times, they were one-time gigs to help someone out — moving furniture for the Production Assistant of a major producer to handing out 8 x 10s at Fan Fair for Alison Krauss. Once I was hired by Billboard to deliver the magazine to "select" businesses as the magazine came hot off the press. These odd jobs seem insignificant, but through them I became friends with many "higher ups" and one of the examples actually introduced me to a lead singer, with whom we went on to get a deal with RCA.

But I also did a few gigs that were everyday types of a jobs. I worked at the Country Music Hall of Fame as a tour guide. At the time the CMF (Country Music Foundation) owned the Historic RCA STUDIO B, which is where Elvis, Eddy Arnold, among many others recorded. So everyday I was able to be in a studio museum, teaching others about the history and even watch them renovate the studio to its original state from back in the late 50's. I also worked in the main building at the Hall of Fame learning about the history of country music. I thought, "Why not get paid for learning the history of what I should already know?"

Through a friend I got a call to go interview for a new job. It was for Starstruck Entertainment, Reba McEntire's company. They were just completing an extraordinary new building on Music Row and needed a mailroom clerk. I interviewed and got the job! This job was one that really helped my career, and to this day I still feel it helped me in ways that are intangible. I am still friends with many of the employees that I got to know while working there and actually now we even collaborate on certain projects!

Also, while in college, a friend of mine worked for a publishing company. We were in a band together and eventually won over one of the song pluggers who allowed us to come in and play for her live in the office. She pulled in one of her hit producer friends to listen to us as well. The band never worked out, but that producer (Doug Johnson) was finishing up a project where they needed a Dobro player for Fan Fair (which is a music festival in Nashville, since renamed the CMA Music Fest). The Wilkinsons' management (Fitzgerald Hartley) called me and hired me over the phone. They went solely off Johnson's recommendation, without even auditioning me! That was the start of my touring career.

I go into great depth with my "jobie jobs" just to illustrate who you may meet along the way. If you are working "in" the business, many opportunities may come your way. *Who knows* who you are going to meet? But we all know you won't meet anyone just sitting at home.

Just think, as you read this, if you are in a public place, the person to your left or right may change your career!

"The lines of preparation and opportunity always intersect."
— *E. Bruno Pirecki (Industry Insider)*

"In the beginning, take every gig, every demo, every wedding. It all adds to your experiences, which build your 'vocabulary'. Also, play all the way from the front row to the back row."
— *Chris Rodriguez (Artist/Musician)*

Note 8: How do I Get Started?

It isn't as difficult as it might seem! Getting started, like anything else, starts with the first step. In this case, it is getting yourself together. Even before you move to a music town. You look at your music objectively, or have someone who will be brutally honest with you. Look at yourself, your abilities, your equipment, your talent, your ambition and your drive. I *promise* you… if you have these six cylinders firing, *nothing* can stop you. In one form or another, you will be successful. I've seen many succeed with only a few of these attributes. Just imagine what they could have done had they really focused on themselves!

Which brings me to a point that I want to confront with you. What is your definition of "successful?" It is a relative term and means something different to everyone. To someone starting out, it may mean make a living as a musician. To a professional musician, it may mean playing certain award or TV shows. To other musicians, it may mean earning a living from residual income and not having to rely on everyday labor for income. Regardless, you must define what it means to you. If you don't, you will become discouraged. Also, do not measure your success by the success or failure of fellow musicians and artists. Define it by what you desire — your goals and dreams.

A few years ago, I fell into this very same trap and it isn't good for any part of your life. You'll get disgruntled and eventually want to just give up. Luckily for me, my mentor brought this to my attention, in a not-so-subtle way (which is why you need a mentor). It was over the phone, but I think if it were in person, he would have been shaking me back and forth to get it through my thick head. But he told me exactly what I'm telling you. There is a good chance that you are already successful and don't even know it, because it hasn't been defined in your mind. *(More on mentoring in Note 24.)*

It all starts with you. Take some time and write down what you want to accomplish. Is it playing three nights a week at a local club? Is it playing in church every Sunday and Wednesday? Is it taking it to the next level and playing in the studio locally? Or is it moving altogether to a larger music town and pursuing it on the national level?

I feel that everything is secondary to this one simple exercise. Only then are you able to move forward. Go very deep and graphic with your desires. After writing it down, go get it laminated and keep it in your wallet or pocket. Look at it everyday. Put it where you keep your money. Every time you buy something, while the clerk is ringing up the sale, look at it and read over your dreams and goals. On those days when you don't want to practice, look at what you have written and remind yourself of your goal. This method is a time-tested method that has worked countless times. There are many people that do not believe this, but they are the ones who are flailing along the path of life.

"To achieve happiness in music, I think you have to be true to who you really are. Success cannot be measured by money or fame. So if you love and believe in what you do, then you are successful."
— *Josh Shilling (Artist/Musician)*

Note 9: Inspiration/Always be Creating and Going 'Out'

As a creative soul, you must *always* be "filling your well" with new ideas, new approaches to your instrument/voice, and just something that deep down inside you makes you want to be better at what you do. As my parents always told me, "Strive for greatness, because there's always someone out there better than you. Chances are, they want to be where you are!" Meaning, if you don't keep improving, they may take your gig.

So, how do you "fill your well?"

One way is to listen to new music. When I say "new," new to you. It may be something that has just been released, or it may be an old Miles Davis or Chet Baker recording that you just discovered.

Side Note: I've found that listening to some of the old jazz horn players is fantastic for any type of lead players. Some of their phrasing and note choices can really open your mind to new licks.

Anytime my musical mind has gotten stale or I seem to be playing the same song over and over, just in a different key, I change up my song list of music I listen to when I'm in the car or at home. I like putting random music in my iPod from stuff I've purchased but never listened deep into the album. It's always a nice surprise to find the "gems" within what you already have. Another way is through websites like Pandora, where you can give them a few artists that you like, and they seek out other artists that are similar. Do whatever it takes to shake up your musical mind.

Another way to "fill your well" is to go out and hear music. You will meet new people and have experiences that can really change your career, especially if you live in Nashville, New York or L.A. In these towns, you may meet a producer, publisher, attorney and/or other musicians who can help your career. As I write this, I got a call last night from an old college buddy. One of his players got sick and asked if I would come play a tune with him. The show is being recorded for a documentary. For me, it is going to be fun to see him and make music. I spent this morning learning the song, which has quite a unique chord progression. It is eclectic and not something I normally play, but it has opened my mind to new licks. I also know that I'll see folks that I know tonight, and I'll probably meet new people and hear great music. That is definitely a benefit of living in Nashville. So tonight, I'm not going with the intention that my music career is going to explode, but I am going with the notion that it will be fun and I'll meet new people.

Lastly, to keep filling your well, always be creating. Experimenting is how you really find new "nuggets" in your gold mine. It isn't a "numbers" game per se, but by creating… and creating…. and creating…. you get better at it — whether you are writing songs, instrumentals, or solos.

Let's break it down: So, there are 52 weeks in a year. Let's say you write a song a week and record it. Good, bad or indifferent, you write/record a song. At the end of the year, you'll have 52 songs. Let's say that 40 of them are horrible! *Hang with me here.* Forty songs are bad, but you still have 12 that are good. But let's say four of them are amazing!

Twelve songs can make an album and with four great ones, you have your "singles," if you will. But in the process you benefitted by creating those 12 good songs and honed your craft as a musician. If you created 52 songs, you bet you will be better at composing, playing and recording. Plus, through this process, you probably called in some of your friends to help you record parts, which has helped them in their experiences. Before you know it, you'll have "created" a whole new you as a musician/producer/writer.

"You can't score a touchdown if you don't know where the end zone is. The point is, how can you make it somewhere if you don't know where you are going? You have to set goals... they can be changed and moved, but you have to set goals and set time to reach those goals. We only have so much time in a day. You have to network; you have to make a plan; you have to put yourself in a position to win. I bought 15 one-dollar lottery tickets in Winter Park, Florida one weekend. I won $10,000! If I hadn't purchased the tickets I would not have won. You have to put yourself in a position to win and be successful. You don't meet that special person never leaving home. You have to be proactive."
— *Jimmy Carter (Industry Insider, not the former President)*

Note 10: Going Out Part 2

Last night I was at a local club here in Nashville, which I wrote about yesterday in Note 9 "Inspiration/ Always be Creating and Going Out." Like most of this book, I lived what I've been preaching. So my night started at the artist's house, which is where we ran through the song. I was still in the dark as to what exactly this event was about. She explained that it is a documentary that Janet Reno had commissioned called, "Song of America." There were 50 songs, of which they had artists from all over the country learn and perform. Last night, Jim Lauderdale, Janis Ian, Tim O'Brien, and a host of other eclectic, well-known artists were there. The song that we performed was from the late 1700s and was encouraging women to become active on the political scene (which was radical back in those days). Both my buddy who called me, and the artist were so happy (and relieved) that I could perform with them on such short notice. We rehearsed a few times through the song, and then went our separate ways to reconnect at the venue.

Once I arrived at the venue, there was a showcase going on from six to seven. A showcase is usually held in a club, sometimes a rehearsal hall, and it features the artist "showcasing" his or her (or them, if it is a band) abilities. Sometimes they can be great and sometimes they can be dreadful. Normally, they'll hire the musicians who played on the album, or hire the "go to" musicians. If the artist is not well known, or certain key elements go awry, the showcase can be a bit depressing. This one was somewhere in the middle. Some key folks were there, but the vibe wasn't. However, lucky for me, Steve Hinson was playing Pedal Steel. He is one of my favorite steel guitarists. So I was able to watch him and really learn from his every guitar lick and tones — great lesson for me. Afterwards, I went up and talked to him about a few steel guitar things. He told me to call him when I get a chance and we'll meet up. I also spoke with the producer of the project, who is a longtime friend of Steve's. I told the producer to give me a shout if Steve could never make a session. You never want to take work away, but every producer has a list of players they call on.

By this time, the camera crew were arriving as were other artists and musicians. On the way in, I saw many friends who I hadn't seen in years, and it's always nice to catch up! Of course, they ribbed me a bit: "The only time I see you is on TV," one artist said. I replied with, "Yeah, yeah… but you have my number too!"

We were third on the bill, so our time came quickly. Diane Sheets (who is a close friend and world-class vocal instructor), one of her clients Dawn Michele (from the CCM Band, FireFlight), and my wife were there in the crowd.

Once we took the stage, I plugged in my Direct Box (LR BAGGS, which works very well with my guitar) and we got sounds. We played a little to make sure we could hear everything. This kind of event is what we normally call "Plug and Play," or "Plug, Play and Pray," because you never know what your monitors will sound like. It's also called "Run and Gun." There are probably another million phrases for it as well. Once we got sounds, I was able to relax and look around the room, seeing friends and family and new folks who were there for the music. It is the time to take a deep breath, relax and then focus on the song at hand. If you do those three simple steps, it allows you to enjoy the moment much more. There have been times where I'm so concentrated on other things… the song ends and it doesn't register that I just played the song. Always enjoy the moment. That is why musicians play music, to experiment with those great moments. This time, I did! Everyone was happy and the song turned out great!

Afterwards, Diane, Dawn, my wife, and I went out for sushi. So for me, it was great to get to know the artist, because you never know when we may work together!

So to Recap: Got a call for a gig at the last minute. Took it... was able to hang out with an old college buddy and play some music. Met a new artist, saw many other friends, musicians and artists, was a part of a documentary commissioned by Janet Reno, and all along had my family and friends there. Plus the artist I played with compensated me! All of this happened simply because I said yes to a gig.

So the question is, right now, what are you saying "no" to that could potentially be a whole new world opened up to you? All it takes is saying yes and following through. That is when opportunities really come your way.

> *"Always play what's right for the song... it's not always about how much or how many notes you can play."*
> — *Tammy Rogers (Artist/Musician)*

Note 11: Physical Appearance

This is usually a touchy subject for most. Hard core musicians will say it doesn't matter, because it's about the music (or should be). Others say it is all about the look, not about the music. Then some are more in the middle and say it's both.

I agree with all three! *How?* Right? I think it varies across genres of music. As I heard a guy say once, "I'm not in the music business… I'm in *show business*! Music is only a small part of it!"

Let me put it this away, say you are a 75-year-old fat man and you are trying to pull off some Britney Spears or Miley Cyrus outfits and dances on stage. Would that be popular? Probably not. However, that same man could stand on a stage and play in many other genres with no issues at all. With his age, it would probably make some of certain music very authentic and believable. I'm not picking on the image of any certain genre, so we'll take it the other way. What if Britney Spears went for a Bluegrass career and wore her slinky outfits and danced around the stage to mountain music? It wouldn't fit.

My point is that for most of us, we are in the middle. Keep in shape, which definitely has its challenges when traveling. Keep your wardrobe up to date. Be well groomed. I've seen incredible musicians *not* get gigs because of their appearance. Unfair? In my book, *definitely!* But it is the reality of the music business (notice I stuck to "music" and not to "show" business).

I'm not writing this section to tell you how to keep up your appearance, I'm just writing to tell you that it is important. You don't have to be a Brad Pitt or Angelina Jolie, but do your best to keep fit. On the road, I either get out and walk, run on the treadmill or use P90X (a video fitness course). It is handy to have an in-room workout so you don't have to rely on the hotel gym or if the weather is nice enough to get outside. The other option is to go to a local gym. I'll tell you from experience, this can get costly very quickly — taxi ride, plus the one-time gym admission (usually $10-$25 for the one visit). If it is important enough to you, you'll find a way.

Eating right on the road is another challenge. Once again, this is not a health book for traveling, but you can go to www. chadjeffers.com and find great readings recommended for these topics.

As for clothes and grooming, it is always helpful to have assistance in this department. The most economical way is to go find about 10 great "show" shirts and a few pairs of cool jeans. Only wear these for show purposes. Use your street clothes for everyday wear. Have someone other than the sales person helping you, although they can be good.

If you need a different look with your hair, go to a new stylist. Sometimes they can give you unbiased options that will go a long way for you.

"My philosophy on dressing for stage for a female: Ask yourself what kind of show you are dressing for. If it's a regular tour concert, some flattering jeans and an interesting top will always work. If you want to wear a simple t-shirt, you can dress it up with a flashy belt or big necklace. I always like to go pretty simple with just a little bit of flash. Boots with tall heels are a must for me because they give a slimmer, taller, more flattering shape overall. And most importantly, darker and more muted tones in your entire outfit is usually the way to go. You don't want to outshine or try to upstage the other performers or the lead singer!"

"If you are dressing for a special promotional event, private party performance, or television taping, your wardrobe should be a little less casual. No jeans; usually a dress or skirt with a dressy top, and once again, you can never go wrong with all black."

"My suitcase is always packed with lots and lots of options, especially if I am on a tour run with a lot of shows. I have been known to have at least 20 shirts, 10 pairs of pants, and 4-5 pairs of shoes to choose

from on some occasions. (plus tons of belts and accesories) The more choices and combinations, the happier I am for not having to repeat the same outfits over and over."
— *Jamelle Fraley (Artist)*

Once again, this note had to be written to state the obvious and to cover the bases to give you the tools you need.

"In Diamond Rio we have a 200 mile re-wear policy.
Don't re-ware a stage shirt inside of 200 miles on consecutive nights.
If fans are crazy enough to drive more than 200 miles
to see the next night's show... they get what they get.
Oh, don't forget, depending on your genetics and diet, a sniff test is
advised so we can all remain friends."
— *Jimmy Olander (Artist/Musician)*

Note 12: Work Hard and Be Nice

I know this sounds like common sense. But I believe if you work hard and be nice to the folks around you, you will have a winning combination. I've been around musicians and crew guys who have only one or the other qualities and it doesn't work. If you take the hardest worker, and he's a great guy but can't work with others and is always pissed off... he won't make it long. You take a guy who is as nice as can be but doesn't want to work... he/she isn't going to make it either. You must have both.

A successful tour manager used to have a sign hanging in his office, "Be nice or go home!" This tour manager was *the* guy for one of country music's biggest artists. Anytime you needed him, he was available and very cordial. To this day, he and I are still close and I think the world of him. And yes, he is still very successful in his "Work Hard and Be Nice" kind of manner.

I heard it put once, if you need someone's help, why wouldn't you be nice to him or her? They are giving you their time, attention and expertise. If you are nice to them, do you think they are more apt to help than if you were a jerk? Of course!

I was in a band where we were playing a festival. The budget was thin, so we were using local sound company help for our monitors. Our drummer somehow had a beef with the monitor guy before the show. So he went over to the monitor guy and gave him a piece of his mind. Through a few word exchanges our guy stomped off and back to his drum kit. To say the least, *none* of our monitors were good that show, and I'm sure it is because of our guy being a jerk to the sound guy. Keep in mind, many of these crew guys were on stage five to 10 hours before we were. They have been setting up all day for us. So it makes no sense to "diss" them. I'm not taking up for the crew guys and yes, it can be frustrating when things aren't right. *But* as a professional, you must believe they are doing their best. Sometimes it may be obvious that they aren't doing their best... however, you must stay strong and do the best you can with what you have. Especially on fairs and festivals. I have found it helpful to go up to the sound crew, introduce myself and ask what I can do to help them. It is a great start in the right direction. They may be jerks, but be nice. I've seen it a hundred times where they'll warm up and help you in a very efficient/effective way.

But working hard also applies to rehearsals. Be there on time, or even better yet, ahead of time to make sure your gear is working properly. There is nothing worse than showing up late, setting up your gear, and finding something is busted in your rig. Everyone is standing there staring at you waiting for you to get it together. Even now that I have guitar techs, I still like to get there and make sure it is the way I want it and sounds the way I want it to sound. It is a small thing, but it makes a huge difference in how the rehearsal/gig goes — work hard and be nice!

> *"In this business, treat people good on your way up,*
> *because you're going to meet them on your way down."*
> — *Tony Stephens (Industry Insider)*

Note 13: It's all About Sales. Are You a Salesman?

In one form or another, we are all in sales. Whether you are asking a girl on a date, selling something at a yard sale, selling your friends on what you want to do on a Friday night, or selling a crowd on you as a musician, it's all sales!

So how do you sell right now as a musician/artist? Do you get on stage and stand in the corner, in the dark and never look up? Or do you take a solo with your toes curled over the front part of the stage (downstage) and really entertain those who came to see you? It doesn't matter whether it is a club of 50 people or a crowd of 50,000. You need to be the entertainer who really sells it! I was always taught on the larger shows to play to the front row. Once you have those folks, everyone else will follow. If you are taking a solo or have an integral part of a song…work it and make it work for you. If the part is easy, make it look hard. If the part is hard, focus on it, but don't let it look hard to those watching. "Why is that?" I hear you ask.

When the part is easy, you can "ham" it up. You aren't making it look difficult for you, you are making it look difficult for anyone else to attempt it. This is when the crowd comes away saying "Wow! He was great and made it look so easy!" On the other hand, if there is a part you need to really focus on and make it right for the song, don't give all the weird looks like you are struggling. Nothing is more painful and awkward for the audience than to see you struggling on a part. It makes them feel uncomfortable.

Don't let your reaction show that it is difficult for you, rather it is just plain difficult for everyone else to play!

Sales is also about putting your best foot forward and being a showman. I filled in a gig with James Otto, who is a class act. At one point of the show, he had us all do a "white man" dance. Well, I'm a white man, but not a dancer. But this skit was meant to be funny. So I used my guitar to add to the dance. He loved it, the crowd loved it, and I got away without having to do a dance. Had I done a "dance," it would be very awkward for everyone in the room, so I found a means around it. No matter what obstacle, there is probably something in your arsenal that you can pull out to make it work. Always look for the "natural" aspect that you can pull off in a pinch.

Sales… let's not pass up the merchandise table (Merch). As an artist especially, you must excel in this. For many startup groups, this is the make or break of their touring. I used to always say, "I'm not a musician; I'm a glorified T-shirt salesman!" When we weren't making much money at the door of clubs, we were making it on the merch. That is where we saw whether we were doing our jobs as entertainers, ahem… salesmen. Most artists use an equation "per head." So if you have 1,000 people in a club and you do $3,000 in merchandise, it is $3 per head. Even the larger acts use that formula.

If you are an artist, after the show, go to the merch table and sign autographs and see your merch sales go up. If for some reason you can't go afterwards, like many festivals where other artists go on right after you, then sign albums and pictures ahead of time. If you sell an album for $20, signed it can be $30. Same with 8 x 10s. If you sell them for $5, signed they can be sold for $10. This is a great way to earn extra income to afford you to tour!

"I interpreted some great advice over lunch with a very successful songwriter as I listened to her complain. Her rant dealt with the 'song' verses the 'will of the musician'. She had a long career working with some of Nashville's greatest musicians. Her rub was, so many times musicians imposed their hottest/favorite licks on her songs without really listening to the lyric and knowing the melody. That seems so rudimentary and simplistic… duh… but often those are the things in life I miss even when they are this blatantly obvious. You will never go wrong by giving more to the song than you do to yourself."
—— *Jimmy Olander (Artist/Musician)*

Note 14: Social Networking

Social Networking is either making your life better or making you scared to death. I know some who have really embraced it, while others push it away and feel it is an invasion of their privacy.

Like most things, if you use it for the right reason, it can benefit you and your career. I have been using both Twitter and Facebook (MySpace to a lesser extent) to help with this book (25 Notes for the Successful Musician). Once you build your base, it is easy for you to inform and update potential fans about your new products. Many more established artists or companies use the bait of a free download for your email, name, city and state.

Bottom line: We are in a new era of information, which determines how we get our information out to consumers. Many musicians (including myself) are using this same mentality to promote themselves for Internet recording. Social networking, if/when you decide to jump in, takes a little time to update and keep current. Always share pictures of you on stage, in the studio or any great moments. I would just try to keep it clean of more personal pictures. I have put a few on mine, but reserved my MySpace for my dog. That is where I post most personal pictures, and family members and friends know the address. It just isn't something I use as a "professional" site.

It is important to update your status for when you are writing, recording, doing promos, working with a new artist/producer, and new musician friends you have made. I see many folks that I haven't seen in a while and they always come up and say, "Man, I hear you have been busy lately writing and recording!" I always respond with, "Yeah, but who told you?" It never fails, they think about it for a minute and then tell me they read it on my Facebook. When you are busy, people want you to be a part of what they are doing. If you are always putting on Facebook… *"Need work. Please, please, please call me!"* It simply won't attract the attention you want, and nine times out of 10, they won't call you. But by Twittering/Facebooking what you are doing, it puts it in folks heads that you are around and working.

I have always believed that most folks in the music business are two years behind touring musicians. It takes a while for word to get around about who's where and what they are doing. I still get folks coming up to me asking if I'm still with Pinmonkey, or Kenny Loggins, or Keith Urban. Carrie did not work much this year (2009), but folks are thinking that I'm gone completely. This is where social networking helps touring musicians spread the word quickly about what they are up to. However, it is a process, and you must build it over time. You can't simply open up a Twitter/Facebook when you are off the road and expect everyone to come to you. You must start *now* and start following and get followers and keep them up to date with your whereabouts!

> *"I came to Nashville to be relevant as a musician and do what I do to the best of my abilities. The talent here is unlike anywhere else in the world. There will always be someone better… much better. So what you have to do is do what you do well and do it with reckless abandon and a great attitude."*
> — Brian Oaks (Producer and Nashville Session Guitarist)

Note 15: Protecting your Personal Life and the Significant Other

There have been times when I had to change my email address, phone number, and report certain information to fan forums. In this age of instant information, you must be careful what information you give out. Even before I went on the road, I got a P.O. Box at the local Post Office. It is cheap, and it is one of the single smartest things I've done. I still have it today, and it is where all of my companies (publishing, studio and production) receive mail.

If you aren't used to this kind of "public-ness," you may ask "Why? What's the big deal?" I've known musicians who woke up on a Saturday morning to a door knock, and it was a fan. Or crazy mail is sent to your house that just doesn't make sense to you. In college, when I worked in the mailroom at Startstruck Entertainment, I would open tons of fan letters. It was interesting to say the least.

Also, on any social media, I'm very careful about what information I post on Twitter and Facebook. Some things just should not be posted for the security of yourself and your family

While on the road, it is smart to keep where you are staying and your room number to yourself. Most musicians don't want a crazy, drunk fan knocking on their hotel door at 4:30 a.m. yelling for them! When on tour, you may stay in a different hotel room every night. Many times tours will workout deals with certain hotels, so it is the *same* hotel, just in a different city! (It messes with your mind sometimes.)

Many people will write their room number on their plastic key card. Which I think that is a bad idea. Two reasons: 1.) If you lose the key and your gear is in your room, you're screwed. 2.) If a fan sees your key card when you are paying for a meal/drink at the hotel bar, they'll know your room. The best trick I've learned is to put your room number in your phone and dial the number and press end. Say your room is 129. Just dial 129, press send, then hang up once it is registered in your phone. Now the trick is not to lose your phone!

If you insist on writing on your key card, I suggest you put the first number last. So, if 129 is your room number, write on your card 291. Whatever the case, just have a system.

As for your spouse, it takes a trust between the two of you for what you do for a living. When you walk on stage and a bunch of girls are screaming for you, yeah, that'll make your spouse a bit uneasy. Make sure your spouse knows that this is all for your future.

When I was with Keith, my wife came to Vegas to see a concert in front of 12,000 or so. It just so happens that night a girl in the same row as my wife had a sign that read, **"I just want a kiss from Chad!"** Of course, Keith read it aloud at one point in the show. All I could do was laugh and probably blush a bit. But my wife thought it was hysterical! Thank goodness she has a sense of humor. The girl with the sign had no idea that my wife was in the same row! We still laugh at that to this day.

Note 16: Is it Music or Business?

This is a touchy subject for some folks. My take is that it is *business*! Of course, it is about the music, but it is still a business. Many look at the music business and have the belief that it is a bunch of good ole boys getting together to jam and have fun. It may be that too, but it is a billion dollar business. So to be successful you must treat it like a business, not a hobby. A hobby is something you do for fun and that's it. Business is something you do to create an income. Sure, it can be fun, but it is business. (Is that point clear yet?)

As a professional musician, you are the *brand*. How you conduct yourself on and off stage is part of your brand. How you dress and what is written on your T-shirt is part of your brand. How you play is part of your brand. The tone of your instrument is part of your brand. The condition of your instrument is part of your brand. Playing in tune is part of your brand. Your stage presence is part of your brand. *Everything* about you is the brand.

Artists spend big dollars to help brand their image. They also protect it very closely, because one "bad" photo could do damage to their brand. I worked with an artist who was sponsored by a bottled water company. So it was imperative for us not to have a competing brand water when we were close to her. One picture of her with this different brand could be detrimental to her endorsement.

When you are on a gig, it is best to keep it professional. This is not to say that you can't be friends with bandmates.

Some of my closest life long friends have been bandmates. However, I've also seen musicians get romantically involved with the artist. Yes, there have been some success stories to that... Reba McEntire did marry her once-upon-a-time steel player, Narvel, who became her manager. Even to this day he has been hugely successful with her career (and with the careers of other artists). But for every success story, there are many more breakups. The breakup more times than not ends the musician's professional relationship with the artist. So one must be careful to not look for a romantic element to further your career. Be professional.

"Music is a business. Music is a product. True. But at its core, Music is art. When we lose sight of that, we lose our soul."
— Wayne Kirkpatrick (Producer/Artist/Musician)

Note 17: Songwriting as a Musician

When I got signed as an artist to RCA, I called up my mentor (Jimmy Olander) to give him the good news. Then I asked, "Now what do I do?" He told me to start writing. I told him that I wasn't a writer. To which he responded, "I don't care, write!" I must say, some of the early writing sessions were rough. I was a true beginner writing with professionals. Songwriting takes some guts, but it's really paid off through the years. Not only have I met some incredible people along the way, it has also brought many studio and live gigs my way. Some of my most notable gigs came from doing work tapes and demos with the co writer. Someone heard them, and in turn recommended me for certain gigs. I've also performed a lot of demo work that was not for my own session. My co writer would say, "You have *got* to play on this song that I wrote a few months ago."

As a musician, if melodies are your strong point, you can really be of value to other writers. I've written with writers who were only lyricists. They didn't sing or play any instrument. So being *a* musician is priceless in that situation. Also, I've found that many writers get in a rut, where they are writing the same song over and over. Same music, different lyrics. It is very valuable to be able to offer substitution chords, which would allow the melody to open up to some new territory. Know that a song is defined as lyrics and melody. So just playing a different chord is not considered "melody." Playing more interesting chords may allow a very interesting, melodic change to take place in the song.

I encourage you to write. Join up with a PRO (Performing Rights Organization). There are only three and you can only join one: ASCAP, BMI and SESAC. Also, joining the NSAI, Nashville Songwriters Association International, is a great way to develop your craft. There are also countless books and videos available.

I have heard that there are a few top session players who were not able to get any session work until they started writing and playing on their own demos. Once producers heard them playing, they inquired on the players. Eventually, their demos lead to work. Instead of pursuing their writing, they were swamped with studio work.

In the music business you never know what is going to be your main asset. It could be songwriting, playing an instrument, maybe you even get into producing; I'd recommend starting with producing your own demos. Or maybe something on the business side, such as a manager, booking agent, selling merchandise fits you more. In a million years, I never thought I would be writing a book about this subject. But it makes sense and the response has been amazing! Believe it or not, through writing this, I have had many new doors open up in areas of the business that have been so helpful. Be open-minded. Being a musician may simply be only one component of your career. This amazing business has so many opportunities.

> *"Take risks... If you win, you will be happy.*
> *If you lose, you will be wise."*
> — *John Spittle (Musician)*

Note 18: Learning New Tunes

This may sound kind of strange, but it will help you greatly.

Understand how you learn songs best. Some people like to make very detailed charts (many use the Nashville Number System); while others would rather make shorthand notes; there are those who would prefer to just memorize. This last one I do not recommend. From both my personal experience and through watching other, more seasoned musicians, I suggest that you prepare a chart of some sort. Through creating the chart, you will memorize the tune. During rehearsals, if the music director/artist wants to take it from the second pre-chorus then straight to the solo, having a chart for reference keeps you better prepared. I have met very few people who never need notes and can still be effective. Even some of the best musicians I've played with have some type of notation.

What works for me is to listen to a bit of the song, and then make a Number Chart. As I comb through the song's guitar licks, I start making notes. After that, I start learning the licks section by section; this is the slowest part for me. Finally, I put it all together. It is so important to be detailed in learning the *correct* notes. During my time playing with Kenny Loggins, he was so amazing at knowing *everyone's* part note for note. I was so overly prepared for that gig, because I had heard of his attention to detail. I'm so glad I was prepared. Being unprepared would have been a bad scene.

A good exercise in learning songs is to take a few songs you really like and chart them out. Study them. Get *your* system down. Also, take some songs from a different genre and learn those too. One painful exercise is to take a few songs that you cannot stand and chart them! Believe it or not, you may have to do this professionally in your career. Playing the music that you prefer to listen to, and playing music professionally can be two different things. I can say that I have been fortunate to make music I enjoy. But we have all been on those gigs, especially when you are first getting started, where you'd just as soon put a bag over your head. Once, I played with an artist in town and I really liked the music. But for some reason, that night this artist was singing about a quarter tone flat! Yikes! At that moment, you just do your job the best you can and hope for the best. Chances are really good that there will be times like this.

One other point I should mention: It is very helpful to learn a few other parts in the songs you are learning. In rehearsal this could be very beneficial to everyone, and there is always that chance on stage where someone's instrument breaks a string, a cable goes bad, or worse yet, the musician passes out! *Who knows?!* But if you know the part, you can jump in!

> *"I guess one thing that helped me was learning how to audition.*
> *I played a lot of auditions unsuccessfully, thinking the artist and*
> *management would see that I could play and that was all I needed*
> *to worry about. It wasn't until I started memorizing the songs that I*
> *started getting gigs. I mean memorizing to the point that I could play*
> *it by myself without vocal or track accompaniment. That's the point*
> *where you can really execute the parts that artists want to hear. Also,*
> *when you're nervous, that level of memorization really helps add to*
> *confidence, which helps calm nerves."*

> *"I'm sure others have their own take on auditioning, but this is what*
> *helped me the most."*

> — *Chas Williams (Author/Musician)*

Note 19: Gear

First off, let me tell you that I *love* gear. Guitars, amps, gadgets, and the new *best* thing! I love it all! But something I learned through the years is to stick with the basics. I'm not saying don't purchase anything new or newly invented, because there are some amazing inventions.

I have spoken with many world-renowned musicians, engineers and producers; they always go back to the basics of gear — for many of us, a great quality guitar with a great quality amp. No tricks, no jive. Just live, the real deal.

I used to always buy the newest greatest piece of gear (which can become a money pit), only to find out, in six months there is something even better. I did this for about five years. Then it sunk in that there will *always* be something new. So, I started buying tried and true pieces of gear, guitars and microphones. Sure there will be something new that I may pick up, but these are the staples of my sound; the signal chain in my studio, and I know how to dial in my sound. When I was purchasing the "new" gear, sometimes it took me forever just to learn how to run the darn thing.

Another note, instead of going out and buying cheaply made units, it is always better to save your money and buy one *great* unit. With technology where it is these days, you can find some inexpensive pieces of gear that are pretty good. But who wants pretty good? Yeah, you sound great and your tone is pretty good. I want it to be **great!** You *and* your tone need to sound ***great!*** Yeah, your song is great, but your tracks are only pretty good. That just won't cut it. So always purchase the best unit/guitar possible.

"Whether you play a vintage instrument, laptop with a controller or somewhere in between, it's important to keep your gear in top working order. You don't want to be the one who's holding up a session, rehearsal or soundcheck, or worse the show (not to mention the evil eyes that might turn your way!). And if your instrument dictates, stay up to date with what's going on technology wise. While it can be financially painful

sometimes, it usually pays off always having the best tools to work with (and don't forget to insure those tools either!)"
— Doug Sisemore (Arranger/Musician)

Note 20: Practicing vs. Rehearsing

This is semantics, but it does need to be mentioned. Practicing is learning, charting, and really getting to know the tune. Many call it "wood shedding" (which means sluggin' it out on your own). Whatever you want to call it, practicing is you and your instrument, learning the song with no one around. I've always been told if someone can hear your playing, you are not practicing, that is called performing.

Rehearsing, on the other hand, is you and the rest of the group/ensemble putting together the pieces that have already been practiced. I've seen a music director almost come unglued because a player had not "practiced" and came to rehearsal completely unprepared. (By the way, that music director was let go a short time after that.) Being prepared is essential in this business. There are enough changing variables. You must be prepared with what can be already learned before getting to rehearsal.

The *only* way to prepare is to spend time with the songs and learn them. Nowadays, I practice with using my DAW (digital audio workstation). I use Protools, which is quite standard, but many use Digital Performer or Logic. It allows me to record. When I listen back, I can hear my part, as well as tone, timing and approach.

The music director may help by sending the songs with the band on one side and the recorded part on the other. This is very helpful so the part is not buried in the mix; it is isolated from the rest of the parts. If the track is *not* separated, you can always put the tracks on one side and the instrument you are practicing on the other. This allows your part to really be heard without turning up the mix.

If you are practicing or rehearsing for a long period of time, **watch the volume!** I know I sound like an old man talking about volume, but playing at high volumes for a long period of time can and will hurt your hearing. Your ears are very necessary for you to function on the professional level. This includes any type of headphones, ear buds and speakers you may use personally.

Anytime I am in an all-day rehearsal, I try to use my in-ear monitors so I can control my volume. Sometimes, if you just use floor monitors (also called wedges), you just do the best you can. I promise you, after the third straight hour of high sound pressure levels (SPLs), your hearing will lose the top frequencies. It may even affect your playing.

One last note on practicing: I have found it helpful to sit and do some "crazy" improvisation on your instrument. Try to do something you've never heard before. It will probably be *very* bad at first, but you may evolve it into something you can actually use in a song.

"Learn and master some sort of digital recording. Build it into your daily routine. Write a song? Record a work tape. Humming a nice

melody? Record a work tape. It's amazing to see how you force yourself to have a better feel, pocket and even tuning when you constantly record yourself. It translates to the stage as well. The tapes won't lie!"
— Granger Smith (Artist)

Note 21: Save (and Invest) Your Money

This seems so basic and fundamental. But it is one of the biggest mistakes I see musicians make. For the typical touring act, you normally work about nine months out of the year. Three months (usually mid December to February or so) is downtime. Basic financial calculations will tell you that if you are not expecting an income during the downtime, you need to have saved money to live on.

Unlike working for a "normal" company or corporate job, where you have a 401k, musicians must independently invest, which takes discipline. Performing professionally is a lot of fun, but one day you *will* need to retire. Your phone may not ring the way it used to for gigs because there is a younger generation working their way into the industry; you need to be prepared.

When I first started my professional career, I had many musicians stress the importance of saving/investing. I'm so indebted to them for that advice. I got so interested in investing, I worked my way through to get my securities license and have been helping area musicians ever since with their finances. The most effective way of investing and saving is to automate your bank account.

The most frequently recommended model for saving and investing is as follows:

Money Market — This is your "rainy day" or emergency fund. This is where you can save for the three down months. It is best to have about six months living expenses in this fund. It is a glorified savings account that will give you a better interest rate.

Medium Term — This is what I usually call the car/guitar fund. This is for purchases three to five years away. Any good growth stock mutual fund will do that and give you 10-12 percent interest.

ROTH IRA — this is your retirement fund. You will not be able to get to this money until you are 59 1/2. Yes it seems far away, but everyday you live, it gets one day closer. You can only put $5,000 in this fund a year, but it grows tax-free. You also cannot make more than $150,000 per year to contribute.

SEP Account — If you have enough "1099" income, you can open an SEP account and contribute to it. This is also for retirement, but also lowers your Adjusted Growth Income (AGI). Lowering your AGI can save you on taxable income and also can allow you to add to your Roth IRA.

If you have kids, it is important to start early on their college fund. Be certain to take care of your Emergency Fund and Retirement first.

Tip: If you are with an artist that performs on TV and/

or award shows, just think of the extra income as your retirement money. Since you typically are not relying on that for your everyday living, just ear mark it to invest as soon as you get it. Years down the road, you'll be glad you did!

A Note About Debt: It is much easier to save when you are debt free. Most folks have a mortgage, which is fine, but unsecured debt such as credit cards, loans and car payments can really put a strain on your finances and relationships. Make it your priority to be debt free.

Legal Note: This publication is designed to provide accurate and authoritative information in regard to the subject mattered covered. It is sold with the understanding that the author and publisher are not engaged in rendering professional services. If professional advice or other expert assistance is required, the services of a competent professional person should be sought.

Note 22: Taxes

This is an area where you must be organized for maximum savings benefits. Personally, while on the road and at home, I save every receipt and keep it in a box. At tax time, I make piles of receipts. (Over the course of the year, my editor puts hers into categorized file folders. Then you save more time when visiting the taxman.) I keep all of my receipts, but put it all on an excel sheet.

Separate your receipts into these categories:

- Supplies/Equipment
- Food and Entertainment
- Clothes (I normally don't count much off because it is a red flag)
- Cell phone
- Home Phone
- Cable/Internet
- Education
- Car Mileage
- Per Diem rates (available at www.irs.gov)
- Postage
- P.O. Box (used only for business)
- Haircuts (only a portion can be used)
- Travel/Hotel
- Shuttles/Parking/Taxis
- Donations
- Union Dues

A quick word about Per Diem (latin for per day). While on tour, allowances are paid out usually by the week, to musicians and crew. $25 to $35/day is common for country music, $50 for rock tours. However, on the irs.gov website, you can see what each individual city is and count the difference off on your taxes.

As opposed to you doing your own taxes, find a great Music Business tax accountant! Tax codes change every year and are very complex. They can help you find money, and that alone pays for their services.

A Note About Buying Gear: When I purchased my studio rig and software to record at home, it started quite the money pit. I'd never buy gear just because it is a tax write off; buy it because you need it and use it.

Legal Note: This publication is designed to provide accurate and authoritative information in regard to the subject mattered covered. It is sold with the understanding that the author and publisher are not engaged in rendering professional services. If professional advice or other expert assistance is required, the services of a competent professional person should be sought.

Note 23: AFM/AFTRA

One mistake that is common among musicians is not understanding the union. There are two main unions for musicians and vocalists. American Federation of Musicians (AFM) is for musicians, and American Federation of Television Radio Association (AFTRA) is for vocalists. If you are a musician who also sings backup, you normally still go through the AFM for many performances. If you do not play an instrument and just sing backup, you will go through AFTRA. The sole purpose of both unions is to help the musician/vocalist get compensated for work done. They also negotiate on behalf of the musician/vocalist the rate of scale. Both unions work to keep the scale of performing live and any media format (radio/TV/Internet) at a fair rate. Most musicians grumble about the AFM and their dues. Dues are a necessary compensation for the unions to stay in business and continue to ensure musicians are compensated appropriately. They also help with filing contracts and track down monies that may be owed to the musician. Other benefits include pension funds, burial insurance, and other insurances that a member can purchase through the union.

It is important to know how to file a contract with the union. **This is so important!** I personally have lost money for not knowing how to correctly fill out the contract. This advice alone is worth what you paid for this book! I have found that many veteran musicians do not know some of the tricks of the trade in filling out the contract. To ensure that this is 100 percent correct, I went to the Union to get it straight "from the horses mouth." Dave Pomeroy, the President of the Nashville Musicians Association, AFM Local 257, has shared some tips regarding filling out the contract to get the maximum compensation available for the work you've done.

Dave Pomeroy: "If you get the paperwork done correctly at the time of the session, it greatly reduces the chance that you will be taken advantage of. You need to make sure the employer you are working for is a signatory company. This means they are in good standing with the AFM. If they aren't and you still work for them, and they don't pay you, you will have a much harder time getting what you are owed. The AFM can help you figure all this out, and once you've done it a few times, it's simple to do, and you will have a paper trail to protect you. If the song you played on gets used elsewhere, like in a movie, TV show or jingle, the Union will make sure you get paid again!"

In terms of dues, it is a hassle and can get expensive, but it *is* a tax write off and ensures that you are getting paid what is owed to you. Hey, if your dues are expensive, that means you're making money!

When doing a media tour (where you perform on many TV shows in a small period of time), keep a record. I always keep track of the show, date we performed, the date it aired, and estimate the dollar amount. Believe it or not, when doing the media tour, you forget when and where you played and money can be lost. I performed on one particular show on one of the major networks. They are known for frequently losing the contracts. They actually told us that we were never there in the studio and that we didn't play on the show! Luckily, we had a copy of our performance. We finally received payment accompanied by a late fee payment that was the same amount as our original check! The more details you have, the better chance you have of tracking down what is owed to you.

Unions have different methods of paying their members. After the venue or producers have reported your performance, the Las Vegas, Nashville and Los Angeles unions will send you the check, and you are responsible in return for paying your dues. The New York unions will notify you of their receipt of your payment with a postcard. It is then up to you to send them your dues and a self-addressed envelope to receive payment.

TIP: In order to get the full benefits on your annual taxes, make copies of each check you write to the union and keep them in a file folder with the rest of your music-related expenses. At tax time, you'll be glad it is altogether.

A great aid to keep track of your performances on TV is to get TiVO. Use the TiVO to schedule recurring tapings of the shows on which you have performed. There have been times when a show is re-aired (which means you get paid residuals) and for whatever reason, payment to the musicians falls through the cracks.

One of the best feelings in the world is when you are sitting at home, flipping through the channels and you see a rerun of a show you are on! You are getting extra exposure and mailbox money (residual income)! I hope you get to experience that someday.

Note 24: Live the Dream and Pass It On!

As I move my career into a different chapter, I feel honored and humbled that many have asked for my advice and help. I must admit that I didn't always feel this way, and neither do many musicians. Most will be very competitive, afraid that you may "steal" a gig from them. I understand that. However, I now realize we are here for a certain purpose. You and your gigs, are simply "yours." Help those around you. No matter where you are in your career, there is someone looking for your guidance, just as you may be seeking guidance from some ahead of you.

If you are able to make music (or anything in the arts) as your means of living, you are living the dream! Even our worst day is what some people would consider their best. Yes, there are challenging times and things aren't always easy. But as long as you keep on keepin' on, helping others and making the best music you can, everything else will take care of itself.

After starting this book, I've been approached to actually coach folks on their career. I've been coaching all along but never in my wildest dreams did I think people would call me to coach. Until my mentor asked me, "If I had a kid that wanted to play basketball professionally, do you think it would be helpful for him to talk to Michael Jordan?" I said, "Well, *yeah!*" He simply said, "That's what aspiring musicians/artists are asking of you. Help them! You can save them a potential five to 10-plus years of their music career by steering them in the right direction. You have lived it and now it is your turn to pass it on!"

I've had the honor of mentoring many artists/musicians, young and old. It is very rewarding and so worthwhile. Regardless of where you are on your musical journey, I strongly encourage you to mentor as well. What you will find is that you will probably learn more than the person you are helping.

I struggled with that conversation. I don't know why. I always want to help others, but just to think that I would be turning a chapter in my professional career to do so was beyond me. But since I have done so, the results are quite amazing. I'm having a blast doing it! Seeing musicians/artists take the next step toward something they never thought was possible, we together are making it possible! You can find more information on this at www.chadjeffers.com. And I ask you to do the same. Take the information from this book and use it. Go do something *big!* After you do so, please write your own book of your experiences and advice. Send me a copy too! It will be different than this book, because you have your own path. But it will still help others. I feel that we are on this earth to help one another.

Live the Dream and Pass it On! Good Luck and All the Best!

Chad Jeffers

Note 25: Random Notes and Questions from Fans

QUESTION: How do you handle everything that comes your way? What do you do when a project or opportunity doesn't go the way you planned or hoped? Like record/songwriting deals?

ANSWER: Early on, I realized the only parts I can control are my thoughts and myself. You can hope all you want that something is going to work out. However, it may work or it may never see the light of day. The same goes for working with other people. You can't control them or their actions. Music is a business, and like many others, you have highs and lows. Regardless of where you are on the "roller coaster," just enjoy it. If you are at a low, learn from it, be positive and fight your way back to a high. The trick is knowing exactly where you are on the roller coaster. Is this a high or a low? Is this a low or is it going lower? Whatever the case, staying focused and goal-oriented is the key. I've worked with folks who are afraid to make and write down goals because they didn't think they could reach them. Well, ya know, they were right.

QUESTION: How is the best way to network?

ANSWER: You have over 1,000 friends in real life and even more on line, how are you effectively leveraging those relationships? There are many secrets to networking. The social media networks online have helped a lot. One of the nicest perks of networking on the Internet is no one can see if you are dressed up or not. Networking is a "blue collar" job. You have to do it when don't want to. I'm constantly looking up friends and colleagues I've played with and reconnecting with them. This is a people business. It is people driven and people make the decisions. Sometimes a simple email of reaching out to someone goes a long way to solidify your relationship.

QUESTION: What is it like living with others on a bus?

ANSWER: There are many times in the music business where you find yourself living on a bus with people you don't know. Getting to know them better really depends on a lot of factors and often puts you outside of your comfort zone. Recently, I went out for two weeks with James Otto. His steel player went on a vacation to see family, so I sub'd for him. No rehearsal, no interaction with hardly knowing anyone. I simply showed up at the bus and introduced myself, and we were off. On the way to the bus, I mentioned to my wife that it's odd that I'm about to go out for four days, live on a 45-foot bus and make music with guys I've never met before. I will say, in this business, you get to know people very well, very quickly.

After you've had the opportunity to get to know the other musicians you're on tour with, it's truly like family. I call it summer camp on wheels. After a few days, everyone knows who's messy, who doesn't flush and who doesn't clean up after themselves. It's pretty much the same on every tour!

QUESTION: How do you know who can be trusted?

ANSWER: There are two ways to look at learning who you can trust out on the road or in the business: 1.) Love and trust everyone, or 2.) Don't trust anyone! I'm in the middle. Most of the time, I lean toward number one, but once you have been burned a few times, you are a bit more cautious in regard to building trust. Fortunately, by now I have created a deep well of friends who have the scoop on many folks I deal with in the business. Sometimes their advice is a bit off, so I often take their advice into consideration and make my own final decision. I've heard *horror* stories about some folks who have turned around and treated me like one of their own. The bottom line is, I go with my instincts. You'll still have disappointments, but it is part of the game.

QUESTION: How is a song written or created? What is the process from conception to it getting recorded?

ANSWER: I view the songwriting process in four steps. You can always in turn, make these steps as complicated or simple as you'd like.

Step 1: Write the tune.

Step 2: Do a guitar/vocal demo, sometimes called work tape. (This is just a rough version of the song.)

Step 3: Out of all of your guitar/vocal demos, find the ones that really stand out and have strong hooks.

Step 4: Demo the great ones

When I am looking to protect and market my songs, I take a
few things under consideration. Technically, once the song is
written it is copyrighted. The problem occurs when someone
says they wrote your song before you did. So to help protect,
you can either do a "poor man's" copyright, in which you
put your lyric sheet and an audio version in a envelope, seal it
in a "non-reseal able" envelope and mail it to yourself. When
you get your own package through the mail, **do not open it.**
The postmark in the unopened package is your protection.

The best way though, is to register it with the Library of
Congress. It costs less than $50 to register. Many songwriters
have an administrator who works on their catalog. They take
care of registering the works and also track down royalties on
behalf of the writer.

There are no written rules for getting your songs heard. Some
writers use song pluggers. These are the guys and girls who get
meetings with labels, producers, attorneys, and even artists to
pitch the tunes. I've heard stories of them running down Faith
Hill in the Green Hills Mall parking lot to give her a tune. (Turns
out, I think she actually cut it!). I personally am out on tour
with many different artists and see many producers. I often have
the opportunity to give the songs directly to them. Regardless,
getting your songs heard is probably the toughest part of getting
the song cut and is getting even more difficult. If you sign a
publishing deal, they have their own pluggers. *Or* if you are like
me and retain your own publishing, you can hire a song plugger.
I've done it all and at the end of the day, it is the same story. *No
one* cares more about your song getting cut than you. *You* are the
best plugger, if you have the connections.

QUESTION: What one piece of advice would you give the musician that has been dedicated to his craft and actively writing and performing in his local scene, of course with the dream of breaking into the business one day?

ANSWER: For starters, you have to do music because you *love it*. That feeling of there is nothing else you can imagine doing but playing/writing music. Like most careers, when you chase money, and not for the love of it, most times you'll burn out. But as for your question, if you really want to get a shot in music on a large scale, you *must* go to where the business is being done. For Country/Christian, it usually is Nashville. For Rock/Pop it is more L.A. or New York. The powers that be will not typically call you in "small town USA." You need to be here and become a part of the fabric of the community. Whether it is as a writer, performer or a player, you must be here. Being located in one of the centers of music is where you'll get gigs and writing appointments.

QUESTION: What has been the most challenging aspect of being an accomplished musician?

ANSWER: For me, it is pushing myself to improve. I am *constantly* buying new music, seeing shows, using Youtube to look for performances — being anywhere where someone is playing an instrument. I'm listening and seeing if there are any techniques I can take away and apply.

Another challenge is to limit pressure and overanalyzing your creative self. You must turn off the "little critic" voice in your head. When you realize that everything you write and create is not going to be perfect, this is when magic can happen.

QUESTION: How easy is it to lose touch with reality once your career takes off? How does one stay grounded?

ANSWER: Surround yourself with good people. Always have a mentor who helps and guides you. And you must be brutally honest with yourself when you feel like you are getting out of control. I think that a little bit of ego is ok... it helps with your self-confidence, as long as you keep it in check. For me, I stay grounded when I realize how much more I have to learn about music and the different instruments that I play. When you surround yourself with the best people in the business, there is a never-ending wealth of knowledge. It's that simple.

QUESTION: How close did your expectations and aspirations of the business match up with the actual experience?

ANSWER: That's a tricky question on many levels. Let's start by saying; I have very high expectations and aspirations. If I didn't, I would never be here now. If you only want to get "kind of good" or do a job somewhat well, then why do it at all? I'm an all or nothing type of guy. Jump in head-first and go for it! Live life with zest and never look back.

There are curve balls that are thrown to you in life that you may just not hit. So when it comes to the actual experience, many times it is different than I expected. But isn't that life? No matter what life you are leading, 10 years ago would you have been able to predict where you are today? Typically not. The decisions along the way shape your destiny. Take for instance, this book. If you told me 10 years ago that I would write a successful book about the unwritten rules of being a musician, I would have laughed! Fifteen years ago, I was learning the business and making my own stupid mistakes. Just as you go along in music, or any business, it is crucial that you make your dreams and goals list. Then, write them down. The process of getting to them may be a curvy road instead of a straight one, but if you have defined the end goal it is more possible to reach.

QUESTION: I've found that accomplished musicians who were huge fans of one particular singer or band can really relate to their own fans' enthusiasms, whereas others just find it bizarre. Would you say that is a fair observation?

ANSWER: I would say that is fair. However, I've never met a musician who wasn't a huge fan of somebody. There is always that one musician/artist/band that comes along that just grabs you and won't let go. I know I've had many of those in my life. I am so grateful for it, because it helps shape me and shows me that my passion is alive and well. Recently, I went to a show that completely rocked my world. Once you work on a tour and have seen hundreds of shows, you build a tolerance for excitement. So when a show or a particular musician comes along that shakes my inner soul, it lets me know that music is still my passion.

Years ago, I heard a story that Elton John went to a CD shop and purchased many random CDs just to listen to new music. In that collection, he purchased Ryan Adams, Gold album. Elton was so inspired by this album, he later said, "that album made me want to write and record again." If someone as seasoned as Elton has this experience, it goes to show that we all need some inspiration from time to time.

QUESTION: Is all the touring and being away really worth it?

ANSWER: Absolutely! To see the smiling faces of many folks when we play and see that they are having a great time makes everything worthwhile. Even though the time between shows can be grueling, the 90-minute performance is the best part of the day.

And of course, we get paid too! What an added bonus!

QUESTION: How do you deal with the lack of privacy?

ANSWER: It's tough, but you deal with it. It does come with the territory. At times you can be paranoid, but the deal is to be on your best behavior, because whether you like it or not, you are representing the artist at all times. People may not say your name, but they'll say, "The guitar player of so and so was a jerk (or very polite)."

You get to the point where you acknowledge strangers as you would someone you know. So many times when I'm out and about, folks will come up to me and say they saw me in Somewhere USA and enjoyed the show. I just go along with it. Some artists/musicians have an ability to remember every person they meet, unfortunately, that's not a skill of mine.

At home, I live a very private life. My wife gets recognized more than I do. Folks will come up to her and say, "Are you Chad Jeffers' wife?"

But one day I was in a drug store and a lady approached me and said, "Hey!" to which I responded, "Oh, hey! How are you!?!" Thinking that this is a fan who has been to a show. So I proceeded... "What has been going on?" She said, "Not much. I'm shopping for a shaver for my son and need a male opinion. Can you help me out?" Uhhhhh, ego buster! So I transformed in 2.5 seconds into a "drug store" clerk to help the lady pick out a good shaver for her son. The funny part is that I hadn't shaved in weeks. Why would she be asking me a question about shaving?

QUESTION: Do you enjoy interacting with fans after a show on the road, or do they interfere with your work, plans, need for sleep, etc.? How important is it for you to have fan support on the road, and do you prefer playing to familiar faces or strangers?

ANSWER: I *love* interacting with Fans. These people are, to a large extent, why I pursued music. Fan support on the road is crucial! It's what keeps us going from day to day. Keep in mind, our day is like the movie "Groundhog Day." Every day is the same. The spice comes from the fans!

QUESTION: Familiar faces or strangers?

ANSWER: *All.* It's what makes our job exciting!

QUESTION: Is there a point where it becomes less of a "fun" thing to do and more of a job? I ask this because I've always had a blast playing, but do some musicians lose sight of the joy and let it become more of a job and less of an art form?

ANSWER: Yes and No. It has been my experience that when it gets to be a 'job' being on stage, it is time to move on to another gig or "shake up" the set a bit. If you are a sideman, it is not your decision. In general, the toughest part of the job is traveling non-stop and living out of a suitcase. Different hotel every night, different city, and then the dreaded airport hassle. I think for most musicians, the best part of the day (and what we look forward to) is being onstage and playing music.

QUESTION: How do you keep yourself grounded in your real life? (Do you have a quote you live by?)

ANSWER: I have a ritual for when I get home, if I have been gone a long time. Typically, it involves being quiet for about an hour, unpack, throw clothes in the laundry, pet my beloved dog, and really just get back to the domestic life. My wife knows that this hour of solitude is much needed time for me. After the hour, I'm truly home. My neighbors joke with me when I do work around the house, "Yeah, Rock Star last week, cleaning gutters this week!" For me, it helps keep me balanced.

As for quotes, we have *many* around the house — on the refrigerator and also written on a chalkboard that I update weekly. My favorite is, "Life isn't about finding yourself. Life is about creating yourself." Author is Unknown.

QUESTION: What made you decide you wanted to live the life?

ANSWER: When I was eight years old, my father (who is also a singer/songwriter) performed at Freedom Hall in Johnson City, TN. My brother and I were his band. The show was in front of 2,500 Rainbow Girls (gorainbow.org) ages 12-18. After the show, they chased my brother and me into the dressing room wanting our autograph. The decision was made at that moment by both of us to always be in music.

Valuable Resources

As a Musician:

American Federation of Musicians afm.org

Nashville	(615) 244-9514	afm257.org
Los Angeles	(323) 462-2161	promusic47.org
New York	(212) 245-4802	local802afm.org
Las Vegas	(702) 647-3690	musicianslasvegas369.com

Sound Recording Special Payments Fund sound-recording.org

The Sound Recording Special Payments Fund (SRSPF), *formerly known as the Phonograph Record Manufacturers' Special Payments Fund,* provides one of the best benefits available to musicians under the collective bargaining agreement between the American Federation of Musicians (AFM) and the recording industry. The SRSPF website was created to provide musicians with information and facts about how the SRSPF works and to offer musicians an easy way to access the details of their prior years distributions or tax reporting and recording session statements. Musicians can also sign up for direct deposit to receive annual distributions or update their change of address or other contact information. All it takes is a few moments to fill out the registration form to become a member of the SRSPF website.

Sound Exchange soundexchange.com

Sound Exchange is an independent, non-profit performance rights organization that is designated by the U.S. Copyright Office to collect and distribute digital performance royalties for featured recording artists and sound recording copyright owners (usually a record label) when their sound recordings are performed on digital cable and satellite television music, internet and satellite radio (such as XM and Sirius). Sound Exchange currently represents over 3,500 record labels and over 31,000 featured artists and whose members include both signed and unsigned recording artists; small, medium and large independent record companies; and major label groups and artist-owned labels.

Instrument Insurance

Marsh Affinity Group Services   afm.org/why-join/u-s-benefits/marsh-affinity-group-services

Music Pro Insurance musicproinsurance.com

Other

Musicians Health musicianshealth.com

Great tips for keeping musician related issues at bay

Entertainment News afm.org/resources/billboard-top-100

Up to date news on what's going on in the business

Harmony Central harmony-central.com

Online forum for musicians and non-bias reviews of products

Sound Matters soundmatters.org

Through the Sound Matters campaign, Starkey Hearing Foundation is raising social awareness of healthy hearing, prevention of hearing damage, and regular hearing check-ups.

MusiCares grammy.com/musicares

MusiCares provides a safety net of critical assistance for music people in times of need. MusiCares' services and resources cover a wide range of financial, medical and personal emergencies, and each case is treated with integrity and confidentiality. MusiCares also focuses the resources and attention of the music industry on human service issues that directly impact the health and welfare of the music community.

As a Songwriter:

Performing Rights Organizations are businesses designed to represent songwriters and publishers and their right to be compensated for having their music performed in public.

ASCAP ascap.com

American Federation of Composers, Authors and Publishers

BMI bmi.com

Broadcast Music Inc.

SESAC sesac.com

Society of European Stage Authors & Composers

NSAI nashvillesongwriters.com

Nashville Songwriters Association International

A.F.M. LOCAL 257 TIME CARD

Card# _____ of _____

Recording	Regular	Special	Low Budget	Live/Location	Video Promo	Limited Pressing	Demo	Overdub	Other				
	☒	☐	☐	☐	☐	☐	☐	☐	☐				

Television Videotape	30 mis.	1 Hour	1.5 Hours	2 Hours	Cable	CMT	National	Local	TV ID	Movie	Other		
	☐	☐	☐	☐	☐	☐	☐	☐	☐	☐			

Radio	30 mis.	1 Hour	1.5 Hours	2 Hours	National	Local	NPR	Syndicated	Other		Motion Pictures	Movie ☐	Individual ☐	Low Assign ☐	Other ☐
	☐	☐	☐	☐	☐	☐	☐	☐	☐						

Jingles	TV	Radio	Both	National	Local	Other
	☐	☐	☐	☐	☐	☐

Other _____

Company __Sony Music Entertainment__   Leader __CHAD JEFFERS__
Signatory (if different) _____   Contractor _____
Billing Address __550 Madison Ave__   Producer __MARK BRIGHT__
__New York, NY 10022__   Production Asst. _____
Phone # __212-833-6785__   Artist/Show/Product __Tony Bennett__
Co. Representative __Keith__   Place of Employment (studio) __Blackbird__
     Address __Berry Hill, TN__

Session Date __5-22-09__   # of Sessions __1__

Session 1	Session 2	Session 3
Start __10 AM__	Start _____	Start _____
End __1 PM__	End _____	End _____

Leader / Contractor Requirements
Fill out the top of this card before musicians sign. This time card becomes a part of the AFM contract. Turn in both copies of the time card to the Local 257 Union office immediately following the session. The second yellow copy will be forwarded to the employer with the contract billing.

	Signature	Social Security #	Doubles (If any)	Obls Rqst Nat Used	Double Scale	Cartage	Cartage Bill rendered or mailed	Local # other than 257	overtime in minutes	Check each session worked 1 2 3
Leader	Chadfll	555-12-5338			☐	☐				☐☐☐
Contractor					☐	☐				☐☐☐
	Craig Krampf				☐	☐				☐☐☐
	Craig Krampf	999-99-9999			☒	☐	☒			☐☐☐
					☐	☐				☐☐☐
					☐	☐				☐☐☐
	Dave Pomeroy	456-78-1234			☐	☐				☐☐☐
					☐	☐				☐☐☐
					☐	☐				☐☐☐

With their signature, members employed certify that the above hours are correct.

Song titles

Session#	Title	length in minutes	Session#	Title	length in minutes
1	"Let it Be"	3:15			
	"Free bird"	8:22			
	"Sweet Home Alabama"	3:10			

Arranger _____ (attach bill)   Copyist _____ (attach bill)

I, the undersigned company representative of this (these) session(s), have reviewed the work represented by this time card and submit this card in lieu of the official contract until said contract is prepared. In the event this time card documents a Demo recording session(s), I agree to the Demo language on the reverse side.

Company Representative __Mark Bright__
__(PRODUCER)__

Audio Demo Recording

1. The Employer/Company recognizes the Local Union as the sole and exclusive collective bargaining agent for all instrumental musicians, conductors, copyists, orchestrators and arrangers of instrumental music, synthesizer programmers, and those who perform similar or related services connected with the recording of Demonstration Recordings within the jurisdiction of the Local Union.

2. The Employer/Company shall not require, request, induce or in any manner attempt to influence any person covered by this Agreement to render services pertaining to the production of Demonstration Recordings except under the terms of this Agreement. The Local Union shall make every effort and exercise full authority to see that its members engaged in recording activities do nothing in derogation of the terms and intent of this Agreement.

3a. The Employer/Company shall give advance notice to the Local Union of all Sessions called under this Agreement, unless services are rendered within the jurisdiction of AFM Local 257, where original time cards must be signed and submitted with this completed B-5 Report Form.

3b. A completed B-5 Report Form (see reverse side) shall be filed and signed by the Employer/Company or its designee with the Local Union and shall accompany each payment required under this Agreement for each recording session.

4. Representatives of the Local Union and/or the Federation shall have access to the place of recording for the purpose of conferring with the musicians.

5. An Employer/Company may sell, assign, lease, license or otherwise transfer title to a recording produced under the terms of this Agreement to any other person, firm or corporation, provided that in advance of any such sale, assignment, lease, license or transfer: (1) the Employer/Company obtains from the other party (buyer, assignee, lessee, licensee or transferee) a Buyer's Assumption Agreement made expressly for the benefit of the American Federation of Musicians as representative of the musicians involved, requiring such buyer, assignee, lessee, licensee or transferee to comply with all the provisions of this Agreement; and (2) the American Federation of Musicians approves in writing the financial responsibility of the buyer, assignee, lessee, licensee or transferee. The Federation shall be deemed to have granted the request to approve the Buyer's Assumption Agreement unless the Federation provides written notice to the contrary within ninety (90) days from the receipt of the request to approve the Buyer's Assumption Agreement.

Once the Buyer's Assumption Agreement goes into effect pursuant to the prior provision, the Employer/Company shall not be liable for any further payments for that particular recording.

6a. Should any recording produced under the auspices of this Agreement ever, without limitation to the duration of this Agreement, be included in any sound recording/digital download, the Employer/Company shall immediately inform the Local Union of that fact and further agrees to enter into and fulfill all conditions required by the then current Sound Recording Labor Agreement of the Federation, together with the Sound Recording Trust Agreement and the Sound Recording Manufacturers' Special Payments Fund Agreement appropriate thereto. Payment of the then prevailing wages, benefits, and payments specified in those agreements shall be made to all Musicians who performed services in the original production of the Demonstration Recording(s), including all provisions for total minutes of music, minimum calls, doubling, etc.

6b. In the event that the recording made under this agreement is ever used for any purpose not explicitly set forth herein, including but not limited to conventions, sound recordings/digital downloads, commercial announcements, motions pictures, television film, videotape/live television, DVD ("New Use"), the Employer/Company shall sign upon presentation and shall fulfill all conditions required by the applicable agreement of the American Federation of Musicians pertaining to such use, including but not limited to payment of all applicable wages and benefits. Said New Use of any specific song or portion thereof recorded under this agreement shall require the payment of all applicable American Federation of Musicians wages and benefits to all original participating musicians, including those performing services on overdub sessions associated with the specific song or portion thereof.

7. Pursuant to the provisions of federal law, in those states where permitted, the Employer/Company agrees to deduct the applicable work dues, based on scale wages, from the wages of each musician rendering services pursuant to this Agreement and to remit such work dues to the Union within 15 days after such deductions are made.

8. Employer/Company agrees to be bound by the Trust Indenture dated 10/2/59, as amended from time to time, providing for contributions to the AFM and Employers' Pension Fund, and further agrees to contribute to such Fund on behalf of the musicians engaged by the Employer/Company, an amount equal to 11% of the Scale Wages earned by said musicians (percentage may be subject to future Sound Recording Labor Agreement negotiations and/or AFM International Executive Board action).

9. To the extent permitted by applicable law, all musicians who are members in good standing of the American Federation of Musicians, hereinafter called the Federation, when their employment commences hereunder shall be continued in such employment only so long as they remain members in good standing of the Federation. All other musicians covered by this Agreement shall become and remain members in good standing of the Federation on or after the thirtieth day following the commencement of their employment or the effective date of this Agreement, whichever is later.

10. Any musicians on this engagement are free to cease service hereunder by reason of any strike, ban, unfair list order or requirement of the Federation or of any Federation local approved or sanctioned by the Federation, and shall be free to accept and engage in other employment of the same or similar character or otherwise, without any restraint, hindrance, penalty, obligation or liability whatever, any other provisions of this contract to the contrary notwithstanding.

11. The Employer/Company represents that there does not exist against it, in favor of any member of the Federation, any claim of any kind arising out of musical services rendered for any such employer. No employee will be required to perform any provisions of this contract or to render any services for said employer as long as any such claim is unsatisfied or unpaid, in whole or in part.

12. The Employer/Company, in signing this contract himself, or having same signed by a representative, acknowledges his (her or their) authority to do so and hereby assumes liability for the amount stated herein, and, if applicable to the services to be rendered hereunder, acknowledges his liability to provide workmen's compensation insurance and to pay social security and unemployment insurance taxes.

13. It is expressly understood and agreed by all the parties hereto that neither the Federation nor any subordinate body thereof is liable for any breach of this agreement by the employer or by any of the employees.

Demonstration Recording Form B-5

Advice to Young Musicians

By
Robert Schumann

Foreword by Chad Jeffers

Foreword

"Advice to Young Musicians" was a book I found a long time ago. At first read, it was hard to understand, because it was written in the late 1800's by Robert Schumann. Like many musicians, he wrote this book as a means to pass on his knowledge.

As you read his quotes, some will sound dated, but the message is still true in today's music world. Let this be a guide that you can refer to often. Many of the quotes will mean something different to you throughout your career; I know it has for me.

May you have a blessed and lasting career in music.

Best

Chad Jeffers

Practice frequently the scale and other finger exercises; but this alone is not sufficient. There are many people who think to obtain grand results in this way, and who up to a mature age spend many hours daily in mechanical labor. That is about the same, as if we tried every day to pronounce the alphabet with greater volubility!

You can employ your time more usefully.

There are such things as mute piano forte-keyboards; try them for a while, and you will discover that they are useless. Dumb people cannot teach us to speak.

Play strictly in time! The playing of many a virtuoso resembles the walk of an intoxicated person. Do not take such as your model.

Learn betimes the fundamental principles of Harmony.

Do not be afraid of the words Theory, Thoroughbass, Counterpoint, etc.; you will understand their full meaning in due time.

Never jingle! Play always with energy and do not leave a piece unfinished.

You may play too slow or too fast; both are faults.

Endeavor to play easy pieces well and with elegance; that is better than to play difficult pieces badly.

Take care always to have your instrument well tuned.

It is not only necessary that you should be able to play your pieces on the instrument, but you should also be able to hum the air without the piano. Strengthen your imagination so, that you may not only retain the melody of a composition, but even the harmony which belongs to it.

Endeavor, even with a poor voice, to sing at first sight without the aid of the instrument; by these means your ear for music will constantly improve: but in case you are endowed with a good voice, do not hesitate a moment to cultivate it; considering it at the same time as the most valuable gift which heaven has granted you!

You must be able to understand a piece of music upon paper.

When you play, never mind who listens to you.

Play always as if in the presence of a master.

If any one should place before you a composition
to play at sight, read it over before you play it.

When you have done your musical day's work and
feel tired, do not exert yourself further. It is better
to rest than to work without pleasure and vigor.

In maturer years play no fashionable trifles. Time
is precious. We should need to live a hundred
lives, only to become acquainted with all the good
works that exist.

With sweetmeats, pastry and confectionary we cannot bring up children in sound health. The mental food must be as simple and nourishing as the bodily. Great composers have sufficiently provided for the former; keep to their works.

All bravura-music soon grows antiquated. Rapid execution is valuable only when used to perfect the performance of real music.

Never help to circulate bad compositions; on the contrary, help to suppress them with earnestness.

You should neither play bad compositions, nor, unless compelled, listen to them.

Do not think velocity, or passage-playing, your highest aim. Try to produce such an impression with a piece of music as was intended by the composer; all further exertions are caricatures.

Think it a vile habit to alter works of good composers, to omit parts of them, or to insert new-fashioned ornaments. This is the greatest insult you can offer to Art.

As to choice in the study of your pieces, ask the advice of more experienced persons than yourself; by so doing, you will save much time.

You must become acquainted by degrees with all the principal works of the more celebrated masters.

Do not be elated by the applause of the multitude; that of artists is of greater value.

All that is merely modish will soon go out of fashion, and if you practice it in age, you will appear a fop whom nobody esteems.

Much playing in society is more injurious than useful. Suit the taste and capacity of your audience; but never play anything which you know is trashy and worthless.

Do not miss an opportunity of practicing music in company with others; as for example in Duets, Trios, etc.; this gives you a flowing and elevated style of playing, and self-possession.--Frequently accompany singers.

If all would play first violin, we could not obtain an orchestra. Therefore esteem every musician in his place.

Love your peculiar instrument, but be not vain enough to consider it the greatest and only one. Remember that there are others as fine as yours. Remember also that singers exist, and that numbers, both in Chorus and Orchestra, produce the most sublime music; therefore do not overrate any Solo.

As you grow up, become more intimate with scores (or partitions) than with virtuosi.

Frequently play the fugues of good masters, above all, those by J. Seb. Bach. Let his "Well-tempered Harpsichord" be your daily bread. By these means you will certainly become a proficient.

Let your intimate friends be chosen from such as are better informed than yourself.

Relieve the severity of your musical studies by reading poetry. Take many a walk in the fields and woods!

From vocalists you may learn much, but do not believe all that they say.

Remember, there are more people in the world than yourself. Be modest! You have not yet invented nor thought anything which others have not thought or invented before. And should you really have done so, consider it a gift of heaven which you are to share with others.

You will be most readily cured of vanity or presumption by studying the history of music, and by hearing the master pieces which have been produced at different periods.

A very valuable book you will find that: On Purity in Music, by Thibaut, a German Professor. Read it often, when you have come to years of greater maturity.

If you pass a church and hear an organ, go in and listen. If allowed to sit on the organ bench, try your inexperienced fingers and marvel at the supreme power of music.

Do not miss an opportunity of practicing on the organ; for there is no instrument that can so effectually correct errors or impurity of style and touch as that.

Frequently sing in choruses, especially the middle parts, this will help to make you a real musician.

What is it to be musical? You will not be so, if your eyes are fixed on the notes with anxiety and you play your piece laboriously through; you will not be so, if (supposing that somebody should turn over two pages at once) you stop short and cannot proceed. But you will be so if you can almost foresee in a new piece what is to follow, or remember it in an old one,--in a word, if you have not only music in your fingers, but also in your head and heart.

But how do we become musical? This, my young friend, is a gift from above; it consists chiefly of a fine ear and quick conception. And these gifts may be cultivated and enhanced. You will not become musical by confining yourself to your room and to mere mechanical studies, but by an extensive intercourse with the musical world, especially with the Chorus and the Orchestra.

Become in early years well informed as to the extent of the human voice in its four modifications.

Attend to it especially in the Chorus, examine in what tones its highest power lies, in what others it can be employed to affect the soft and tender passions.

Pay attention to national airs and songs of the people; they contain a vast assemblage of the finest melodies, and open to you a glimpse of the character of the different nations.

Fail not to practise the reading of old clefs, otherwise many treasures of past times will remain a closed fountain to you.

Attend early to the tone and character of the various instruments; try to impress their peculiar sound on your ear.

Do not neglect to attend good Operas.

Highly esteem the Old, but take also a warm interest in the New. Be not prejudiced against names unknown to you.

Do not judge a composition from the first time of hearing; that which pleases you at the first moment, is not always the best. Masters need to be studied. Many things will not become clear to you till you have reached a more advanced age.

In judging of compositions, discriminate between works of real art and those merely calculated to amuse amateurs. Cherish those of the former description, and do not get angry with the others.

Melody is the battle-cry of amateurs, and certainly

music without melody is nothing. Understand, however, what these persons mean by it: a simple, flowing and pleasing rhythmical tune; this is enough to satisfy them.

There are, however, others of a different sort, and whenever you open Bach, Mozart, Beethoven, or any real master, their melodies meet you in a thousand different shapes. I trust you will soon be tired of the inferior melodies, especially those out of the new Italian operas; and of all vulgar ones.

If, while at the piano, you attempt to form little melodies, that is very well; but if they come into your mind of themselves, when you are not practising, you may be still more pleased; for the internal organ of music is then roused in you. The fingers must do what the head desires; not the contrary.

If you begin to compose, work it out in your head. Do not try a piece on your instrument, except when you have fully conceived it. If your music came from your heart and soul, and did you feel it yourself,--it will operate on others in the same manner.

If Heaven has bestowed on you a fine imagination, you will often be seated at your piano in solitary hours, as if attached to it; you will desire to express the feelings of your heart in harmony, and the more clouded the sphere of harmony may perhaps be to you, the more mysteriously you will feel as if drawn into magic circles.

In youth these may be your happiest hours. Beware, however, of abandoning yourself too often to the influence of a talent that induces you to lavish powers and time, as it were, upon phantoms. Mastery over the forms of composition and a clear expression of your ideas can only be attained by constant writing. Write, therefore, more than you improvise.

Acquire an early knowledge of the art of conducting music. Observe often the best conductors, and conduct along with them in your mind. This will give you clearness of perception and make you accurate.

Look deeply into life, and study it as diligently as the other arts and sciences.

The laws of morals are those of art.

By means of industry and perseverance you will rise higher and higher.

From a pound of iron, that costs little, a thousand watch-springs can be made, whose value becomes prodigious. The pound you have received from the Lord,--use it faithfully.

Without enthusiasm nothing great can be effected in art.

The object of art is not to produce riches. Become a great artist, and all other desirable accessories will fall to your lot.

The Spirit will not become clear to you, before you understand the Forms of composition.

Perhaps genius alone understands genius fully.

It has been thought that a perfect musician must be able to see, in his mind's eye, any new, and even complicated, piece of orchestral music as if in full score lying before him! This is indeed the greatest triumph of musical intellect that can be imagined.

There is no end of learning.

Made in the USA
Monee, IL
02 December 2019